# Médée

Pierre Corneille's Medea (1635) in English Translation

Translated by Susan Kalter

Corneille, Pierre, 1606-1684.
    Pierre Corneille's Médée.

    Translation of Médée.

    1. Médée (Greek mythology)—Drama. I. Kalter, Susan. II. Title.

# CONTENTS

# Translator's Note

This American English free verse translation was created from the French version, available through Wikisource the free library at

https://fr.wikisource.org/wiki/*Médée*_(Corneille) .

It was originally created for the sole purpose of teaching to undergraduates in the absence of any other available English-language translations.

In an era of crowdsourcing, translations no longer have to be an endeavor undertaken by a solitary translator working with a small team of editors and reviewers. This translator invites readers to contact her if they find "blunders and infelicities" (as Eric Korn wrote of his drafts for his translation of Racine's *Andromache*, published in 1988), though allowance should be made for a modicum of creative license here and there, such as the tripling of the adjective describing the Furies in Act I, Scene IV. Please email advice and corrections to smkalte@yahoo.com toward a second, corrected edition.

I hope that this version will also make an acceptable though imperfect text for theatrical production. All inquiries about possible performances should be addressed to Department of English, Illinois State University, Normal, IL 61790-4240.

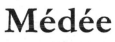

# Médée

by
Pierre Corneille

# CHARACTERS

**Créon**, king of Corinth.
**Ægée**, king of Athens.
**Jason**, Médée's husband.
**Pollux**, Argonaut, friend of Jason.
**Créuse**, Créon's daughter.
**Médée**, Jason's wife.
**Cléone**, Créuse's governess.
**Nérine**, Médée's follower.
**Theudas**, Créon's servant.
TROOP OF THE GUARDS OF CRÉON.

*The scene is Corinth.*

# ACT I.

## Scene the first.

*Pollux, Jason.*

### Pollux.

How I feel all at once both surprise and joy!
Can it be that I finally see you again in these parts,
That Pollux in Corinth has met with Jason?

### Jason.

You could not come here in a better season;
And to astonish your soul still more,
Prepare yourself to behold my second nuptials.

### Pollux.

What! So Médée is dead, my friend?

### Jason.

            No, she lives;
But a lovelier object chases her from my bed.

### Pollux.

Gods! and what will she do?

### Jason.

          And what did Hypsipyle do,
But shoot forth the blazing splinters of a useless wrath?          10
She hurled cries, she shed tears,
She wished upon me thousands upon thousands of misfortunes;
Said that I was faithless, heartless, without conscience,
And weary of saying it, she took patience.
Médée in her misfortune will be able to do as much:
How she sighs, cries, and names me inconstant;
I leave her with regret, but I have no alibi
Against a greater power who gives me to Créuse.

9

### Pollux.

So Créuse is the object who has just now inflamed you?
I would have guessed it without having heard her named.     20
Jason never took common mistresses;
He was born solely to charm princesses,
And would hate love, if it had under its law
Arranged for lesser hearts than the daughters of kings.
Hypsipyle at Lemnos, on the Phasis[1] Médée,
And Créuse at Corinth, so much worth, possessed,
Does well to show that in all places, without the succor of Mars,
Sceptres are acquired with his slightest glance.

### Jason.

Likewise I am not one of those vulgar lovers;
I accommodate the flame of my passion to the good of my affairs;   30
And under some clime that fate throws to me,
By maxim of State I make this effort for myself.
Wanting at Lemnos to refresh ourselves in the town,
What would we have done, Pollux, without the love of Hypsipyle?
And later at Colchos, what did your Jason else,
But cajole Médée and win the fleece?
Thus, without my love, what would your valor have accomplished?
Would it have lured the dragon from his vigilance?
Those people begotten of the earth fully armed,
Which of you would have defeated them, if Jason had not loved?   40
Now that an exile forbids from me my homeland,
Créuse is the subject of my idolatry;
And I found the finesse, in paying her court,
To lift my fate on the wings of Love.

### Pollux.

How do you speak of exile? The hatred of Pélie...

### Jason.

Forces me, even in death, to flee his Thessaly.

### Pollux.

He is dead!

## Jason.

Listen, and you will know how
His demise alone obliges me to this estrangement.
After six years passed, since our voyage,
In the greatest pleasures that one tastes of marriage,                    50
My father, terribly fragile, moving me to pity,
I conjured² Médée, in the name of friendship…

## Pollux.

I knew how her art, forcing destinies,³
Restored to him the vigor of his younger years:
It was, if I remember, here that I learned it;
Whence suddenly a voyage to Asia undertaken
Made it so that, our two sojourns divided by Neptune,
I knew not since what your fortunes had been;
I am only just arrived.

## Jason.

Learn then from me
The subject that obliges me to break faith with her.                    60
Despite the aversion between our two families,
Of my tyrant Pélie⁴ she wins over the daughters,
And feigns to them on my part so many outrages received,
That these weak spirits are easily deceived.
She makes friendship, promises them marvels,
With the power of her art fills their ears;
And to better demonstrate to them how infinite it is,
Flaunts chiefly before them my father rejuvenated.
For proof she slits the throat of a ram in their sight,
Plunges him into a bath of water and herbs unknown,                    70
Forms for him a new blood with this liqueur,
And renders him the size and the vigor of a lamb.
The sisters cry miracle, and each one delighted
Conceives for her old father a like envy,
Wants a like effect, asks for it, and obtains it;
But each one has her purpose. However the night comes:
Médée, after the stroke of such a beautiful lure,
Prepares pure water and herbs without force,

Redoubles the sleep of the guards and the king:
The result just to recount makes me tremble with horror.
With pity their ally these inhumane daughters
From their father asleep go to drain the blood from his veins:
Their gullible tenderness, through great thrustings of knives,
Gives too prodigally this old blood, to make room for the new;
The most mortal blow is imputed to be a great service;
They call this cruel sacrifice piety;
And paternal love which makes their arms act
Would believe it committing a crime not to commit one.
To give them courage Médée is eloquent:
Each one nevertheless turns aside her face;
A secret horror condemns their design,
And their eyes refuse to guide their hand.

### Pollux.

To represent to me this tragic spectacle,
Which makes a parricide and promises a miracle,
I feel horror myself, and cannot conceive
That a spirit thus far lets itself be deceived.

### Jason.

Thus my father Eson recovered his youth,
But hear the rest.  This great courage ceases;
Horror seizes them; Médée jeers at them, and flees.
Day discovers to all the crimes of the night;
And to spare you pointless chatter,
Acaste,[5] the new king, causes the city to mutiny,
Names Jason the author of this treason,
And to avenge his father lays siege to my house.
But I was already far gone, as was Médée;
And my family finally reaching Corinth,
We salute Créon, whose benignity
Promises us against Acaste a place of security.
What more will I tell you? my ordinary good fortune
Acquires for me the wills of the daughter and father;
So well that both equally cherished,
The one wants me for his son-in-law, and the other for husband.

The sovereign splendors of a crownèd rival
The majesty of Ægée, and the sceptre of Athens,
Have nothing, in their view, comparable to me,
And banished as I am, I am more to them than a king.
I see too clearly this good fortune, but I conceal it;
And although for Créuse a like fire burns in me,
With conjugal duty I combat my love,
And I only nourish it to make my court.[6]                                    120
Acaste meanwhile threatens war
Which must lose Créon and unpeople his land;
Then, changing all of a sudden his resolves,
He proposes peace under certain conditions.
He demands first both Jason and Médée:
They refuse him the one, and the other is granted;
I impede it, they debate, and I work such,
That finally it is reduced to her banishment.
Again I hinder it, and Créon refuses me;
And to console me for it he offers me his Créuse                              130
What was I to have done, Pollux, in this extremity
Which was committing my life with my loyalty?
For no doubt to risk the useful for the honest,
Peace was going to be made at the expense of my head;
Insolent contempt of the offers of a great king
Into the hands of an enemy was delivering Médée and myself.
I would have done it however, if I had not been a father,
The love of my children made my soul light;
My loss was theirs; and these new nuptials
Pull them from the tomb with Médée and myself.                               140
They alone made me resolve, and the peace was concluded.

### Pollux.

Although on all sides the affair is resolved
Leaving no place to the advice of a friend,
Yet I can approve it only halfway.
On whatsoever you base a treatment so rude,
It is to show for Médée a little ingratitude;
What she did for you is poorly recompensed.
One must fear after all her courage offended:
You know better than I what her charms can do.

#### Jason.

They are for her fury terrifying weapons;
But her banishment will guarantee us.

#### Pollux.

Take care not to have cause to repent of it.

#### Jason.

Although it might happen, friend, it is a done deal.

#### Pollux.

May the heavens conclude it as I wish it!
Permit however that in order to acquit myself,
I go to find the king to congratulate him on it.

#### Jason.

I would guide you there, but I await my princess
Who will be coming out of the temple.

#### Pollux.

                              Adieu:  love presses you,
And I would be sorry that an officious care
Should make you lose on my account such precious time.          160

## Scene II.

#### Jason.

Since my spirit became capable of catching fire,
Never a like trouble confounded my soul.
My heart, which is shared between two affections,
Lets itself be torn into a thousand passions.
I owe all to Médée, and I cannot without shame
Both of her and of my faith take so little account:
I owe all to Créon, and of such a powerful king
I make an enemy, if I keep my faith:

I regret Médée, and I worship Créuse;
I see my crime in the one, in the other my excuse;          170
And on top of my regret my desires triumphant
Have still the rescue of the care for my children.[7]
But the princess comes; the radiance of such a face
From the most constant in the world would attract homage,
And seems to reproach my fidelity
To have dared hold out against such beauty.

## Scene III.

*Jason, Créuse, Cléone.*

### Jason.

How long your zeal is, and how it gives impatience
To your lover, who dies in your absence!

### Créuse.

Yet I did not make to heaven many wishes;
Having Jason to myself, I have all that I want.          180

### Jason.

And myself, may I hope the effect of a prayer
That the flame of my passion would be held in singular favor?
In the name of our love, save two young fruits
That from a first nuptial the bed produced for me;
Employ yourself for them, attach them to a father
That they be not taken up in the exile of their mother;
It is her alone who banishes these little unfortunates,
Since in the treaties there is no word of them.

### Créuse.

I have already had pity on their tender innocence,
And will serve you there with all my power,          190
Provided that in your turn you accord me one point
That, until a little while hence, I will mention not to you.

## Jason.

Tell, and whatever it may be, how my queen has it at her disposal.

## Créuse.

If I can from my father obtain something,
You will know it afterward; I want nothing for nothing.

## Cléone.

You will be able at the palace to follow this negotiation.
They open at the house of Médée, remove yourself from her sight;
Your presence would bring back her pain the more moved,
And you would be sorry that that jealous spirit
Was mixing her bitterness with pleasures so tender.                    200

# Scene IV.

## Médée.

Sovereign guardians of the laws of Hymen,[8]
Gods guarantor of the faith that Jason gave me,
You that he called to witness an ardor immortal
When by a false oath he vanquished my modesty,
See with what contempt his perjury treats you,
And help me to avenge this common insult:
If he can chase me away today with impunity,
You are without power or without resentment.
And you, wise, knowing, learnèd troop in black barbarity,
Daughters of the Acheron,[9] plagues, larvae, Furies,[10]                    210
Proud sisters, if ever our narrow commerce
On you and your serpents gave me any right,
Come out from your dungeons with the same flames
And the same torments with which you trouble souls;
Let them a while repose in their irons;
The better to act for me make truce in hell.
Bring to me from the bottom of the lair of Mégère[11]
The death of my rival, and that of her father,
And if you do not want to serve my wrath poorly,
Something worse for my perfidious spouse:                    220

May he run vagabond from province to province,
May he cowardly pay court to each prince;
Banished on all sides, without property or support,
Oppressed by fear, misery, boredom,
May none commiserate his greatest misfortunes;
May his last torture be to regret me;[12]
And until he rests in the tomb may the memory of me
Attach to his spirit an eternal torment.
Jason repudiate me! and who would have been able to believe it?
If he lacked love, does he lack memory?                                    230
Can he well leave me after so many benefactions?
Dare he well leave me after so many felonies?
Knowing what I can do, having seen what I dare,
Does he believe that to offend me is so small a thing?
What! my father betrayed, the elements compelled,
The limbs of a brother scattered in the sea,
Do they cause him to presume my audacity exhausted?
Do they cause him to presume that in my turn scorned,
My rage against him has no way to be gratified,
And that all my power is limited to serving him?                           240
Thou abusest thyself, Jason, I am still myself.
All that in thy favor my extreme love did,
I will do it out of hatred; and I want at the very least
That a felony separate us, as it joined us;
That my bloody divorce, in murders, in carnage,
Is equal to the first days of our marriage,
And that our union, which thine alteration ruptures,
Finds an end like unto its beginning.
To tear apart morsel by morsel the child before the eyes of the father
Is but the least effect that will follow my choler;                        250
Crimes so light were my trial blows:
It must well be shown otherwise what I know,
I must make a masterpiece, and a last work that
Surpasses by far this feeble apprenticeship.
But to execute all that I undertake,
Which gods will furnish me with succor large enough?
It is no longer you, hell, that here I solicit:
Your fires are impotent for what I meditate.
Author of my birth, as well as of the day,
That regretfully thou dispense upon this fatal residence,                  260

17

Sun, who sees the affront that they are going to do to thy race,
Give me thy horses to steer in your place:
Grant this grace to my scorching desire.
I want to fall on Corinth with your burning chariot:
But fear not the descent to the fatal universe;
Corinth consumed will guarantee the rest;
From my just wrath the implacable vows
Will contain your fires within its odious walls.
Créon there is prince, and takes Jason for son-in-law:
It is enough to merit it be reduced to cinders,                        270
To see there reduced all the isthmus, in order to punish him for it,
And that it prevent no longer the two seas from uniting.


## Scene V.

*Médée, Nérine.*


### Médée.

Ah well! Nérine, when, when these nuptials?
Have they chosen the hour? dost thou know the day?
Didst thou learn nothing? didst thou see not Jason?
Does he apprehend nothing after his betrayal?
Does he believe that at this affront, I amuse myself in complaining?
If he ceases to love me, may he begin to fear me.
He will see, the perfidious one, to what height of horror
Can the fury rise from my resentments.                                 280


### Nérine.

Moderate the broths of this violence,
And let your sufferings be disguised in silence.
What! madame, is this the way that one needs to dissimulate?
And need one scatter thereby the menacings into the air?
The most ardent transports of a known hate
Are only so much aborted lightning in the cloud,
So much forewarning to those you want to punish,
To repulse your blows, or to avert them.
Who can without being moved endure an offense,
Can better take to its moment the time of her vengeance;               290

And her feigned sweetness, under a mortal allurement,
Leads her victim insensibly to the altar.

### Médée.

Thou wantest me to be quiet and to dissimulate!
Nérine, carry elsewhere this ridiculous counsel:
The soul is incapable of it under the least misfortunes,
And has nowhere to hide such grief.
Jason made me betray my country and my father,
And leaves me in the midst of a foreign land,
With no support, no friends, no retreat, no property,
The fable of his people and the hatred of mine:                300
Nérine, after that thou wantest me to be quiet!
Shall I not furthermore in testimony to the ease,
Of this royal nuptial wish the happy day,
And force all my cares to serve his love?

### Nérine.

Madame, think better on the outburst that you make
However just it may be, look where you are;
Consider that scarcely a spirit more pardoning
Holds you in security among your enemies.

### Médée.

The soul must stiffen the more it is threatened,
And against fortune to go head lowered,                        310
Shock it boldly, and without fearing death
Present itself abreast of its unkindest effort.
This cowardly enemy fears great braveries,
And on those that she fells redoubles her outrages.

### Nérine.

What does this great bravery serve where the one has no power?

### Médée.

It always finds occasion to make the most of itself.

#### Nérine.

Force the blindness by which you are seduced,
To see in what state fate has you reduced.
Your country hates you, your spouse is faithless:
In such a grand reversal what remains for you?

#### Médée.

Myself,        320
Myself, say I, and that is enough.

#### Nérine.

What! you alone, madame?

#### Médée.

Yes, thou seest in myself alone both fire and flame,
Both earth, and sea, both hell, and heaven,
Both sceptre of the kings, and thunderbolt of the gods.

#### Nérine.

The impetuous ardor of a courage sensible
To your resentments imagines all possible:
But you must fear a king strong with so many subjects.

#### Médée.

My father, who was that king, did he break up my schemes?

#### Nérine.

No; but he was surprised, and Créon mistrusts.
Flee, that to his suspicions he not sacrifice you.    330

#### Médée.

Alas! I have fled only too much; this infidelity
With a just chastisement punishes my cowardice.
If I had fled not for the death of Pélie,
If I had held fast within Thessaly,
He had never seen Créuse, and this new object
Would of our nuptials have snuffed not the torch.

### Nérine.

Flee again, I beg you.

### Médée.

Yes, I will flee, Nérine;
But, first, of Créon we will see the ruin.
I brave fortune, and all its rigor
In ousting a husband from me does not oust my heart; 340
Be faithful only, and without putting thyself to trouble,
Let my knowledge and my hate act fully.

### Nérine, *alone.*

Madame...She leaves me instead of listening to me,
These violent transports will hurl her down,
From too just an ardor the inexorable envy
Makes her abandon concern for her life.
Let us try again a blow to divert the course.
To appease her fury, is to conserve her days.

END OF THE FIRST ACT.

# ACT II.

## Scene the first.

*Médée, Nérine.*

### Nérine.

Although a certain peril follows your undertaking,
Be assured of me, I belong fully to you;                      350
Use my service up to flames, up to poison,
I refuse nothing; but spare Jason.
Your blind vengeance once quenched,
Regret for his death will cost you your life;
And the violent blows of a rigorous weariness...[13]

### Médée.

Cease to speak to me of it and fear not for him:
My fury to that extreme would not dare seduce me;
Jason has cost me too much to want to destroy him;
My wrath takes mercy on him, and my first ardor
Sustains his interest at the core of my heart.             360
I believe that he loves me still, and that he nourishes in his soul
Some secret remains of a flame so beautiful, so passionate,
That he means only to obey the will of a king
Who tears him from Médée in spite of his faith.
May he live, and if still possible, may the ingrate stay with me;
If not, it is enough for me if his Créuse dies;
May he live however, and enjoy the day
That preserves for him still my undying love.
Créon alone and his daughter committed the perfidy!
They alone will round out all the tragedy;                  370
Their loss will conclude this fatal peace.

### Nérine.

Contain yourself, madame; he is exiting his palace.

## Scene II.

*Créon, Médée, Nérine, soldiers.*

### Créon.

What! I see thee again! With what impudence
Canst thou, without being frightened, support my presence?
Art thou unaware of the judgment ordering thy banishment?
Dost thou value my authority so little?
See how she puffs herself up with both pride and audacity!
Her eyes are none but fire; her look, what menace!
Guards, keep her away from me.
Go, purge my States of a monster such as thou;                    380
Deliver my subjects and myself from fear.

### Médée.

Of what am I accused? What crime, what complaint
For my banishment gives you so much ardor?

### Créon.

Ah! Innocence itself! Candor itself!
Médée is a mirror of signal virtue:
What inhumanity to have exiled her!
Barbarian, hast thou so soon forgotten so many horrors?
Look back over thy felonies, look back over thine errors,
And out of so many countries name one district
To which thy wickedness permits thee entrée.                      390
All Thessaly in arms pursues thee;
Thy father detests thee, and the universe flees from thee:
Must I in favor of thee load upon myself so many hatreds,
Both on my people and myself make fall thy afflictions?
Go practice elsewhere thy black actions;
I bought back peace under these conditions.

### Médée.

Coward peace, that between you, without having listened to me
To tear my property from me you plotted!
Peace, for which the dishonor rests eternally upon you!

23

Whosoever without hearing her condemns a criminal,                    400
His crime had it a hundred times merited the punishment,
Of a just chastisement he makes an injustice.

### Créon.

With comparison to Pélie, he was much better treated;
Before slitting his throat thou had listened to him?

### Médée.

Did he listen to Jason, when his covert hatred
Sent him onto our borders to surrender himself to his destruction?
For what do you want me to call a plan
Greater than his strength and the power of humankind?
Learn what was this illustrious conquest,
And with how many dead I guaranteed his head.                        410
We had to put to the yoke two furious bulls;
Maelstroms of fire were rushing forth from their eyes,
And their master Vulcan was sending forth by their exhalations
A conflagration lengthening over all the plain;
Having tamed them, we entered into new dangers;
We had to plow the sad fields of Mars,
And with the teeth of a serpent sow their land,
Whose sterility, fertile for war,
Was producing at that instant cadres armed
Against the same hand which had sown them.                           420
But, whatever a perfect valor did against them,
The fleece was not at the end of their defeat:
A dragon, drunk on the most mortal poisons
That begot the sins of all the seasons,
Vomiting a thousand shafts of lightning from his inflamed throat,
Was guarding it much better than all that army;
Never star, moon, aurora nor sun,
Saw his eyelid lowered in sleep:
I lulled him to sleep alone; alone, I through my charms
Placed in the yoke the bulls, and undid the gendarmes.               430
If at the time to my duty my limited desire
Had kept my glory and my fidelity,
If I felt horror at so many enormous transgressions,

24

What would have become of Jason, and all your Argonauts?
Without me, this valiant chief, whom you ravished from me,
Would have perished first, and all would have followed him.
I repent not to have by my skill
Saved the blood of the gods and the flower of Greece:
Zéthès, and Calaïs, and Pollux, and Castor,
And the charming Orphée, and the sage Nestor,[14]          440
All your heroes ultimately owe their life to me;
I will see you possess them all without envy.
I saved them for you, I cede them all to you;
I want but one for myself, be not jealous of it.
For such good results leave me the infidel:
It is my sole crime, if I am criminal;
To love this inconstant one, is all that I did:
If you punish me, give me back my felony.
Is it to employ as it must be a legitimate power,
To make me culpable and to enjoy my crime?          450

### Créon.

Go, thee, complain at Colchos.

### Médée.

                    Returning there will please me.
May Jason deliver me there again just as he pulled me away:
I am ready to leave under the same escort
Who from those beloved parts precipitated my flight.
O from an unjust affront the most cruel blows!
You make a difference between two criminals!
You want them to honor him, and that of two accomplices
The one have your crown, and the other tortures!

### Créon.

Cease from now on to mix thine interest with his.
Thy Jason, taken aside, is too much a man of good:          460
Separating him from thee, his defense is easy;
Never did he betray his father nor his city;
Never innocent blood stained red his hands;
Never lent he his arms to thy designs;

His crime, if he has one, is to have thee for wife.
Let him free himself from a shameful flame of passion;
Give him back his innocence by removing thyself from us;
Carry to other climes thine insolent wrath;
Thine herbs, thy poisons, thy heart without pity,
And all that which ever made Jason guilty. 470

### Médée.

Paint my actions blacker than night;
I have only shame for them, he has all the fruit;
It was on his behalf that my audacious wisdom
Immolated his tyrant by the hands of his own race;
Add there my country and my brother: it suffices
That none of so many evils go but to his profit.
But you knew them all when you received me;
Your simplicity has been not deceived:
Did you not know one of them when you promised me
A rampart certain against mine enemies? 480
My hand, bloody still from the murder of Pélie,
Raised against me all of Thessaly,
When your heart, sensible to compassion,
Despite all my felonies, undertook my protection.
If the one can impute some crime to me since,
It is too small that exile, my death be legitimate:
If not, to what purpose do you treat me thus?
I am guilty elsewhere, but innocent here.

### Créon.

I want no more here of such an innocence,
Nor to suffer in my court thy fatal presence. 490
Go…

### Médée.

Just gods, avengers…

### Créon.

Go, I say, to other parts
Through thy cries importunate solicit the gods.

Leave us thy children: I would be too severe,
If I punished them for the crimes of their mother;
And although I might do it with just reason,
My daughter asks for them on behalf of Jason.

## Médée.

Barbarous humanity, who uproots me, tears me from myself,
And pretends gentleness to remove from me what I love!
If Jason and Créuse thus ordained it,
May they give me back the blood that I gave them.                    500

## Créon.

Answer me no more, follow the law which is made for thee;
Prepare thy departure, and think to thy retreat.
To deliberate about it, and chose the quarter,
With grace my kindness gives thee a full day.

## Médée.

What grace!

## Créon.

                    Soldiers, bring her back home;
Her appeal would become eternal.
*(Médée returns home, and Creon continues.)*
What an indomitable spirit! What an arrogant bearing
Accompanied the pride of so long a conversation!
Did she bow none from her haughty mood?
Was she able to condescend to the slightest prayer?                    510
And the sacred respect of my status
Did she from it extract any submission?

## Scene III.

*Créon, Jason, Créuse, Cléone, soldiers.*

### Créon.

There thou art without rival, and my country without wars,
My daughter: it is tomorrow that she leaves our lands.
We have from now on to fear only on her part;
Acaste is satisfied with such a near departure;
And if thou canst calm the courage of Ægée,
Who sees through our choice his ardor neglected,
Make report that tomorrow assures us forever
Both within and without a profound peace.                    520

### Créuse.

I do not believe, sire, that that old king of Athens,
Seeing in the hands of others the fruit of so many pains,
Mixes so much weakness with his resentment,
That his initial wrath dissipates easily.
I hope nevertheless that with a little skill
I will resolve him to lose a mistress
Whose indecent age and inclination
Responded poorly enough to his affection.

### Jason.

He must testify to you by his obedience
How much over his spirit you have power;                    530
And if he remains obstinate in following an unjust wrath,
We will know, my princess, how to put down its blows;
And our preparations against Thessaly
Have too much wherewithal to punish the flame and folly of his
    passion.

### Créon.

We will not come to that: look only
To pay him esteem and thanks.
I would like for any other a little raillery;
An old man amorous deserves one to laugh at it:

But the throne sustains the majesty of kings
Above contempt, as above the laws.                                    540
One owes always respect to the sceptre, to the crown.
Rely for all, if thou wantest, on the orders that I give;
I'll know how to appease him with facility,
If only thou acquit thyself with civility.

## Scene IV.

*Jason, Créuse, Cléone.*

### Jason.

What do I not owe to you for this preference,
Where my desires dared not carry my hope!
It is heartily to testify to me an infinite love,
To scorn a king for a banished pauper!
To all his grandeur to prefer my misery!
To turn in my favor the will of a father!                             550
To secure my children against a rigorous exile!

### Créuse.

What less was a loving courage able to do?
Fortune showed within your birth
A stroke of her longing, or of her impotence;
She owed a sceptre to the blood from which you are born,
And without her your virtues merited it enough.
Love, which was unable to see such an injustice,
Made up for her defect, or punished her malice,
And gives you, at the height of your adversities,
The sceptre that I await, and that you deserve.                        560
Glory remains for me in it; and future races,
Counting on our nuptials between your adventures,[15]
Will vaunt forever my generous love,
Which ruptures the unfortunate fate of such a great hero.
After all, however, laugh at my weakness;
Ready to possess the phoenix of Greece,
The flower of our warriors, the blood of so many gods,
The gown of Médée struck my eyes;

My caprice, to its lustre attaching my longing,
Though she finds herself unwilling to wish good fortune on
    my life; 570
It is what my exalted designs claimed,
For the price of the children that I saved for you.

Jason.

How light is this price for such a good service!
Nevertheless one must employ artifice there:
My jealous one in fury is not a woman to suffer
That my hand despoil her of it to offer it to you;
Of all the treasures for which her father exhausts Scythia,
It is all that she took when she left there.

Créuse.

What a beautiful choice she made! never like brilliance
Sowed in the night the brightness of the sun; 580
The pearls with gold confusingly mixed,
A thousand priceless stones of a divine mélange,
Spaced along its borders dazzle the eyes;
Never anything approaching it is made in these parts.
For myself, as soon as I saw her adorned in it,
I took no more account of the golden fleece;
And must you yourself be a little jealous of it,
I had almost wanted it as soon as you.
To appease Médée and to repair her loss,
The reserves of my father entirely open 590
Place at her abandon all the treasures of the king,
Provided that this gown and Jason be mine.

Jason.

Doubt it not, my queen, it is acquired for you.
I am going to look for Nérine, and by her intervention
To obtain from Médée with dexterity
What her galled courage would refuse.
As for her, you know that I flee from her approaches,
I would feel pain to suffer the pride of her reproaches;
And I know myself badly, or in our conversation

Her wrath arousing itself would arouse mine. 600
I have not a spirit complaisant to her rage,
So far as to support without retort an outrage;
And it would be for me an eternal displeasure
To postpone in this way the result of your desires.
But without further ado, I am going to seize the time
When Nérine will exit from a neighboring house.
Suffer, to advance your contentment,
That despite my love I leave you a moment.

### Cléone.

Madame, I perceive the king of Athens approaching.

### Créuse.

Go then, seeing you will add to his sufferings. 610

### Cléone.

Remember the air with which you must treat him.

### Créuse.

My mouth will know how to acquit itself courteously.

## Scene V.

*Ægée, Créuse, Cléone.*

### Ægée.

Upon a rumor that stuns me, and that I cannot believe,
Madame, my love, jealous for your glory,
Comes to know if it is true that you be consenting,
By a shameful nuptial, to sentence me to death.
Your people tremble at it, your court murmurs of it;
And all of Corinth finally imputes great insult to itself
That a fugitive, a traitor, a murderer of kings,
Gives himself henceforth princes and laws; 620
They cannot endure that the horror of Greece
For price of his felonies espouses their princess,

And that he must add to your titles of honor:
« Wife of an assassin and a poisoner. »

Créuse.

Let reason act, great king, on your soul,
And charge him not with the crimes of his wife.
I espouse, and my father consents to it, an unfortunate one,
But prince, but valiant, and especially innocent.
Not that I err in this preference;
Between your rank and his I know the difference:     630
But if you know love and its ardors,
Ever for its object it does not take majesty;
Confess that its fire wants only majesty of the person,
And that in me you would love nothing less than my crown.
    Often I know not what, that one cannot express,
surprises us, carries us away, and forces us to love;
And often, without reason, the objects of our passionate flames
Strike our eyes harmoniously and seize our souls.
Thus you saw the sovereign of the gods,[16]
In contempt of Juno, love in these base parts,     640
Vénus leave her Mars and neglect her prize,
At one time for Adonis, and another for Anchise;[17]
And it is perhaps still with less reason
That, although you loved me, I give myself to Jason.
At first in my spirit you had this share:
I esteemed you more, and I loved him more.

Ægée.

Keep these compliments for one less inflamed,
And esteem me not that in so far as you love me.
What does this confession of a willful error serve me?
If you believe yourself to err, who forces you to do it?     650
Accuse not love nor its blindness;
When one knows her fault, one fails doubly.

Créuse.

Since therefore you find mine inexcusable,
I want no more, sire, to confess myself guilty.

Love of my country and the good of the State
Forbad me marriage with such a great potentate.
I would have had suddenly to follow you to your provinces,
And deprive my subjects of the sight of their princes.
For me your sceptre is but a pompous exile;
What does its brilliance serve me? and what does it give me?          660
Does it elevate me to a rank higher than sovereign?
And without possessing it do I not see myself queen?
Thanks to the immortals, in my condition
I have the wherewithal to quench me of this ambition:
I want not to exchange my sceptre for another;
I would lose my crown in accepting yours.
Corinth is a good subject, but it wants to see its king,
And would reject the law of a distant prince.
Join to these reasons that a father a little over the age,
At which my sole presence softens his widowerhood,          670
Would not know how to resolve to separate from her
The hope and support of his feeble years,
And recognize that I prefer to you
Only the good of the State, my country and my father.
There is what obliges me to choose another spouse;
But as these reasons have little effect on you,
In order to give back repose to your soul,
Suffer me to leave you.

Ægée, alone.

Go, go, madame,
Expose your allurements and vaunt your contempt
To the infamous sorcerer who charms your spirits.          680
Of this indignity make a bad story;
Laugh at my ardor, laugh at your shame;
Favor he of all your courtiers
Who will jeer the best at the decline of my years;
You will enjoy very little such insolence;
My outraged love courts violence;
My vessels at the harbor, near enough to the port,
Have only too many soldiers to exert a strike.
Youth I lack, but not courage:
Kings lose not force with age;          690

33

And we will see, perhaps before this day is done,
My passion avenged and your pride punished.

END OF THE SECOND ACT.

# ACT III.

## Scene the first.

### Nérine.

Unfortunate instrument of the misfortune which presses down upon
    us,
How I pitied thee, deplorable princess!
Before the sun has made another round,
Thy inevitable loss consummates thy love.
Thy destiny betrays thee, and thy fatal beauty
Under the allurements of a nuptial feast exposes thee to thy rival;
Thy sceptre is impotent to vanquish her effort;
And the day of her flight is the day of thy death.     700
Her vengeance at hand she has only to resolve,
A word from the heavens on high brings down the thunderbolt,
The seas, to drown all, await only her law;
The earth offers to open itself up under the palace of the king;
The air holds back the winds all ready to be led forth by her choler,
So much nature enslaved fears to displease her;
And if all the elements are not enough,
The hells are going to emerge at her commands.
Myself, although my duty attaches me to her service,
I lend her regretfully a complicit silence;     710
From a laudable desire my heart enticed against its will
Would joyfully commit against her an infidelity:
But far from arresting her, her rage discovered,
To that of Créuse would add my loss;
And my fatal advice[18] would serve nothing more
Than to confound my blood in the broth of hers.
By a movement contrary to the movement of my soul,
Fear of death removes from me fear of blame;
And my timidity strives to advance through
That which were it not for the peril I would want to cross.     720

## Scene II.

*Jason, Nérine.*

#### Jason.

Nérine, ah well, what says our exiled one, what does she?
By thy dear conversation is she consoled?
Does she want to cede fully to necessity?

#### Nérine.

I find in her chagrin less animosity;
From moment to moment her soul more humane
Lessens her choler, and reduces her hate:
Already her displeasure no more wishes you ill.

#### Jason.

Make her acquire for all an equal sentiment.
Thee, who knew the tenderness of my love,
Thou canst also know what pain presses down upon me.          730
I feel my heart rend at her departure:
Créuse even takes some share of her misfortunes,
Her tears ran for it; even Créon sighs,
Regretfully prefers the good of his empire to her
And prefers if in her farewell her heart less galled
Wanted to merit the liberality of it;
If Médée was appeasing his threats thus far,
That she had care to depart with his good graces,
I know (as he is good) that his treasures open
To her without reserve would be entirely offered,          740
And despite the misfortunes to which fate reduced her,
Would relieve her pain and support her in her flight.

#### Nérine.

Since she must resolve herself to this banishment,
It is necessary to soften her malcontentedness with it.
This offer can serve to do so; and by it I hope,
With a little skill, to appease her anger
But, otherwise, nevertheless await nothing from me,

If she must take leave of Créuse and of the king;
The object of your love and of her jealousy
Would have soon seized her again with all her fury.                    750

## Jason.

To show her courage appeased without her seeing them,
I will tell thee, Nérine, a method quite easy;
And for such a long time I have known thy prudence,
That without difficulty I confide it to thee entirely.
Créon banishes Médée, and his precise orders
In her banishment engulfed her sons:
The pity of Créuse did so much to her father,
That they will have no part in the misfortune of their mother.
For them she owes her some gratitude;
May a present on her behalf succeed their kind regards:                 760
Her gown, whose brilliance is unbecoming in her fortune,
And in her exile but an importunate burden,
Would win her the heart of a liberal prince,
And the general abandon of all his treasures.
From a vain adornment, useless in her distress,
She can acquire the wherewithal to make herself a queen:[19]
Créuse, or I am mistaken, has some desire for it,
And I do not think that she could have chosen better.
But here she is coming out towards us; suffer me to evade her:
Encountering me troubles her, and my sight galls her.                   770


## Scene III.

*Médée, Jason, Nérine.*

## Médée.

Flee not, Jason, from these baneful places.
It is for me to depart from them:  receive my adieus.
Accustomed to fleeing, exile is a small thing for me;
Its severity for me is once again only in its cause.
It is for you that I fly, it is you who chase me.
Where will you see me again, if you banish me?
Will I go onto the Phasis, where I betrayed my father,

To appease by my blood the manes[20] of my brother?
Will I go to Thessaly, where the murder of a king
Today for victim demands only me?                                              780
There is no clime for which my fatal love
Has not acquired to my name general hatred;
And what did, for you, my knowledge and my hand
Made me an enemy of all humankind.
Remember it again, ingrate; put thyself back on the plain
That these hideous bulls were scorching with their exhalations;
See again this field of war whose sacred furrows
Were rising against thee in sudden battalions;
This dragon whose eyelids never closed
And then prefer Créuse to me, if thou darest.                                  790
What did I spare since then that was in my power?
Did I in accordance with love listen to my duty?
To throw an obstacle into the ardent pursuit
By which my father in fury was already touching thy flight,[21]
Did I sow with regret my brother morsel by morsel?
At this fatal object spread out over the waters,
My father too susceptible to the rights of nature,
Left all other cares but his sepulchre;
And by this new crime moving his pity,
I arrested the effects of his enmity.                                          800
Prodigal of my blood, shame of my family,
As cruel a sister as disloyal a daughter,
These glorious titles were pleasing to my loves;
I took them without horror to preserve thy days.
Then, certainly, then my merit was rare;
Thou wast ashamed not of a barbarous wife.
When to thy father worn-out I restored vigor,
I had still thy vows, I had still thy heart;
But this affection dying with Pélie,
In the same tomb saw itself buried alive:                                      810
Ingratitude in the soul and impudence to my face,
A Scythian in thy bed was to thee now an affront;
And me, whom thy desires had so much wished,
The dragon made sleepy, the fleece carried away,
Thy tyrant massacred, thy father rejuvenated,
I became an object worthy of being banished.
Thy designs achieved, I was worthy of thy hatred,

It was needful to thee to escape a shameful chain,
And take a half[22] who has nothing more than I,
Than the royal circlet[23] that I left for thee.

### Jason.

Ah! yet hast thou of the eyes to read into my soul,
And to see the pure motives of my new flame!
The tender sentiments of a fatherly love
To save my children renders me criminal,
If one can name an unfortunate divorce crime,
To which the care that I have of them reduces and forces me.
Thyself, furious woman, did I do little for thee
In wrenching thy demise from the vengeances of a king?
Without me thine insolence was going to be punished;
At my prayer alone they have only banished thee. 830
It is to reciprocate for the great blows thou hast exerted for me:[24]
Thou saved my life, and I avert thy death.

### Médée.

They have only banished me! o sovereign goodness!
Then it is a favor, and not a penalty!
I receive a grace in lieu of a chastisement!
And my exile yet owes a gratitude!
So the avaricious thirst of the brigand quenched,
It is imputed to mercy that he leave us alive;
When he slits not throats, he believes himself to pardon us,
And what he does not take away, he thinks to give. 840

### Jason.

Thy talk, through which Créon receives more and more offense,
Would force him at last to some violence.
Distance thyself from here while it is still permitted:
Kings are never feeble enemies.

### Médée.

Through thy advice I see well enough thy ruse;
Thou givest it there to me only on behalf of Créuse.
Thy love, disguised by an officious care,
Wants to relieve its eyes of an importunate object.

### Jason.

Call not love an inevitable change,
Which Créuse makes less than the fate which oppresses me.            850

### Médée.

Canst thou well, without blushing, disavow the fires of thy passion?

### Jason.

Ah well, so be it; her attractions take all my vows hostage:
Thou, whom a furtive love soiled with so many crimes,
Darest thou reproach me for legitimate[25] ardors?

### Médée.

Yes, I reproach thee for them, and more...

### Jason.

                                        Which felonies?

### Médée.

Treason, murder and all those that I did.

### Jason.

Missing yet is this point about my deplorable fate,
Which of thy cruelties one might make me guilty.

### Médée.

Thou presumest in vain to take cover from them;
That one does the crime for whom the crime serves.            860
As each one, indignant against those crimes of thy wife,
Treats her in his speech as wicked and infamous,
Thyself alone, for whom her felonies made all his good fortune,
Do hold her for innocent and defend her honor.

### Jason.

I am ashamed of my life, and I hate its exercise,
Since I owe it to the effects of thy rage.

## Médée.

Generous shame, and high virtue!
If thou hatest it so much, why dost thou guard it?

## Jason.

For the good of our children, whose feeble and tender age
Against so many misfortunes would not know how to
    defend itself:                         870
Do become on their behalf of a gentler nature.

## Médée.

My soul at the subject of them redoubles its wrath,
Must this dishonor complete my miseries,
That to my children Créuse at last gives brothers?
Thou art going to mix, impious one, and place on the same rung
Nephews of Sisyphus with those of the Sun!

## Jason.

Their majesty will sustain the fortune of the others;
Créuse and her children will preserve ours.

## Médée.

I will fully prevent it, this odious mélange,
Which together dishonors my race and the gods.       880

## Jason.

Weary of so many evils, let us cede ourselves to fortune.

## Médée.

This body does not enclose such a common soul;
I never suffered her to make the law for me,
And always my fortune depended upon myself.[26]

## Jason.

The fear that I have of a sceptre...

#### Médée.

Ah! heart filled with sham,
Thou masketh thy desires behind a false title of fear;
A sceptre is the sole object that makes thy new choice.

#### Jason.

Dost thou want me to expose myself to the hatred of two kings
And that my imprudence draw down on our heads,
From one direction and another, new tempests?                890

#### Médée.

Flee them, flee them both, follow Médée in thy turn,
And keep at least thy faith, if thou hast no more love.

#### Jason.

It is effortless to fly, but it is not easy
Against two embittered kings to find an exile.
Who will resist them, if they happen to unite?

#### Médée.

Who will resist me, if I want to punish thee,
Disloyal one?  Next to them fear thee so little Médée?
May all their power, with overwhelming weaponry,
Compete against me for thy heart that they surprised from me,
And thou be of the combat both the judge and the prize!          900
Unite them, if thou wantest it, my father and Scythia,
In myself alone they will have only too strong a detachment.
Limitest thou my power to that of humans?
'Gainst them, when it pleases me, I arm their very own hands;
Thou knowest it, thou sawest it, when these sons of the Earth
By their mutual blows ended their war.
Miserable one! I can soften the wrath of bulls;
Flame obeys me, and I command the waters;
Hell trembles, and the heavens, so soon as I name them,
And can I not touch the will of a man!²⁷                 910
I love thee still, Jason, despite thy cowardice;
I am offended no longer by thy frivolity:

I feel my choler decrease at thy glances;
From moment to moment my fury moderates;
And I run without regret toward my banishment,
Since I see come out of it thine establishment.
I have nothing more to ask next but a favor:
Suffer that my children accompany me in my flight;
May I yet admire thee in each of their features,
May I love thee and kiss thee through these little portraits;                920
And may their dear object, preserving my passionate flame,
Present thyself to mine eyes as well as to my soul.

### Jason.

Ah! reinvigorate thine anger, it is less rigorous.
To kidnap my children from me, is to uproot my heart,
And Jupiter all ready to crush me with the thunderbolt,
My demise at hand, could not resolve me to allow it.
It is for them that I change;[28] and Fate, without them,
Alone could cut the knot of our nuptials.[29]

### Médée.

This paternal love, which furnishes thee excuses,
Makes me endure also that thou refuseth me them,                930
I press thee no more about it; and ready to banish myself,
I want no more of thee than a faint memory.

### Jason.

Thy virtuous love made for my greatest glory;
It would be to betray myself to lose that memory:
And mine toward thee, which remains eternal,
Leaves thee in this adieu its solemn oath.
Let strokes most severe shatter my chief
May the great gods set in motion the bitterest fits of choler;
May they unite together to punish me,
If I lose not life before thy memory!                940

## Scene IV.

*Médée, Nérine.*

### Médée.

I will give good order to it; it is in thy power
To forget my love, but not my vengeance;
I will know how to carve it upon thine icy spirits
By strokes too profound to be effaced.
He loves his children, that inflexible, courageous one:
His weakness is discovered; for them he is sensible,
By them my arm, armed with a just rigor,
Will find the routes by which to pierce his heart.

### Nérine.

Madame, spare them, spare the issue of your loins;
Advance not in this way your own extinction:                950
Against an innocent blood why become inflamed,
If Créuse into your lakes happens to be hurled?
She herself throws herself there, and Jason delivers her up to you.

### Médée.

Thou gratify my desires.

### Nérine.

May I cease to live,
If what I tell you is no pure truth!

### Médée.

Ah! hold no longer then my soul in perplexity!

### Nérine.

Madame, we must guard against someone seeing us,
And from the palace of the king discovering our glee:
A design made public rarely succeeds.

### Médée.

Let's return then, and place our secrets under lock and key.        960

END OF THE THIRD ACT.

44

# ACT IV.

## Scene the first.

*Médée, Nérine.*

Médée, *alone in her magic grotto.*[30]

It is too little of Jason that thine eye steals from me,
It is too little of my bed, thou wantest yet my gown,
Insatiable rival; and it is still too little,
If, force at hand, thou hast it without my consent;
It must be that through myself it be offered to thee,
That losing my children, I buy still their loss;
There needs to be an homage in it to thy divine attractions,
And gratitude for the robbery that thou dost to me.
Thou wilt have it; my refusal would be a new crime:
But I intend to adorn thee with it as my victim,                              970
And under a false semblance of liberality,
To make drunk, both my vengeance, and thine avidity.
The charm[31] is completed, thou mayst enter, Nérine.
*(Nérine enters, and Médée continues.)*
My ailments in these poisons find their medicine:
See how serpents at my commandment
From Africa to here have tarried but a moment,
And constrained to obey my baneful charms,
Have on this fatal gift spit out all their pestilence.
Love to all my senses was never so tender
As this sad instrument to my jealous spirit.                                  980
These herbs are not of a common virtue;
I myself in gathering them made the moon turn pale,
When, hair streaming, arm and foot naked,
I despoiled once upon a time an unknown clime of them.
See a thousand other venoms: this thick liquor
Mixes the blood of the hydra with that of Nesse;[32]
Python had this tongue; and this black plumage
Is that which a harpy in fleeing let fall;
By this firebrand Althée[33] quenched her fury,
Too pitiable sister and too cruel mother;                                      990
This fire fell from the sky with Phaéthon,
This other comes with the torrents of the stony Phlégéthon;[34]

And this one of old filled in our own regions
From the sulphurous throats of the bulls of Vulcan.
Finally, thou seest there powders, roots, waters,
Whose the mortal power opens a thousand tombs;
This deceptive present drank their whole force,
And, much better that my arm, will avenge my divorce.
My tyrants by their loss will learn that never…
But whence comes this great noise that I hear from the direction of
    the palace? 1000

Nérine.

From the good fortune of Jason and the misfortune of Ægée:
Madame, just as well, that he had avenged you.
This elderly general, not being able to support
That they swindle from him in his eyes that which he believed he
    deserved,
And that over his crown and his perseverance
The exile of your spouse was the preference,
Endeavored by force to repulse the affront
With which these new nuptials confront him.
As this beauty, for him all ice,
On the shores of the sea was contemplating its tranquility, 1010
He saw her poorly escorted, and took advantage of such a beautiful
    time
To render his desires and yours content.
Of his best soldiers a choice troop
Surrounds the princess, and serves his jealousy;
The terror which surprises her throws her into swoon;
And all that she can do, is to call for Jason.
His guards at first make some resistance,
And the people lend them a weak assistance;
But the light obstacle of these feeble hearts
Shamefully left Créuse to her conquerors: 1020
Already almost at their border she was abducted …

Médée.

I divine the end, my traitor saved her.

### Nérine.

Yes, madame, and what is more Ægée is prisoner;
Your spouse to his myrtle adds this laurel:
But learn how.

### Médée

Speak no more of it:
I want not to know what made his courage;
It suffices that his arm worked for us,
And returned a victim to my just wrath.
Nérine, my sufferings would have little allegiance,
If this abduction saved her from my vengeance;                    1030
To quit her country is one unfortunate therein?
It is not her exile, it is her death that I want;
She would have too much honor to have only my penalty,
And to shed tears for being twice queen.
So many invisible fires enclosed in this gift,
That by a title more true I call my ransom,
Will produce effects far sweeter to my hate.

### Nérine.

In this way you avenge yourself, and her loss is certain:
But against the fury of her father provoked
Where do you think to find a place of security?                   1040

### Médée.

If the prison of Ægée followed his defeat,
Thou canst see that in opening it I open for myself a retreat,
And that his irons smashed, despite their offences,
Toward my protection engage his States.
Only hurry, and run toward my rival
Bring her on my behalf this fatal gown:
Lead my children to her, and have them, if thou canst,
Presented by their father to the object of his wishes.

### Nérine.

But, madame, to bring this gown infested,
That with so many poisons you infected, 1050
It is for your Nérine too deadly an employ:
Before on Créuse they would act on me.

### Médée.

Fear not their virtue, my charm moderates it,
And keeps it from acting except on her and her father;
Such a grand effect takes a heart more hardy,
And without talking back to me, do what I tell thee.

## Scène II.

*Créon, Pollux, soldiers.*

### Créon.

We must fully cherish this perfect valor
That gives us the defeat over our kidnappers.
Invincible heroes, it is to your succor
That I owe henceforth the good fortune of my days; 1060
It is you alone today whose avenging hand
Returns to Créon his daughter, to Jason his mistress,
Puts Ægée in prison and his pride in the dungeon,
And has the earth chewing on his best soldiers.

### Pollux.

Great king, the happy success of this deliverance
Is much better owed to you than to the little valiance I showed:
It is you alone and Jason, whose arms indomitable
Struck death with terror in all directions;
Like two lions whose ardent fury
Empty in a moment an entire sheepfold. 1070
The glorious example of your more-than-human feats
Overheated my courage and guided my hands:
I followed, but from afar, actions so gorgeous,
That were leaving to my arm just so many illustrious models.

Could one draw back in fighting under you,
And have not heart to second your blows?

Créon.

Your valor, which suffers in this retort,
Ousts all belief in your modesty:
But since the refusal of an honor merited
Is not a small trait of generosity,                        1080
I let you enjoy it  Author of the victory,
Just as it will please you, depart from here in glory;
As it is your right, you can give it.
How prudently the gods know how to ordain all!
See, brave warrior, how your arrival
To the day of our misfortunes finds itself reserved,
And how at the point that fate was daring to menace us,
They sent us the means to crush it down.
Worthy blood of their king, demi-god magnanimous,
Whose virtue cannot receive too much esteem,              1090
What have we more to fear? and what jealous destiny,
So long as we will have you, would dare to take after us?

Pollux.

Be apprehensive yet, great prince,

Créon.

Of what?

Pollux.

Médée,
Who sees herself by you of her bed dispossessed.
I fear that it be difficult for you to prevent
A valorous son-in-law from costing you quite dearly.
After the assassination of a monarch and a brother,
Can it be blood that she spares or revers?
Accustomed to murder, and knowing in poisons,
See what she did to acquire Jason;                        1100
And do not presume, whatever Jason tells you,
That to keep him she shall be less hardy.

49

#### Créon.

Of that my spirit is no more disquieted;
By her banishment I made my security;
She has only fury and vengeance in her soul,
But, in so little time, what can a woman do?
I prescribed but one day hence as the appointed time for her
  departure.

#### Pollux.

It is little for a woman, and much for her art;
Against human powers do not measure charms.

#### Créon.

However powerful they may be, I feel no alarm;                    1110
And even if this delay should hazard all,
My word is given, and I intend to keep it.

## Scene III.

*Créon, Pollux, Cléone.*

#### Créon.

What are our two lovers up to, Cléone?

#### Cléone.

                              The princess,
Liege, near to Jason recaptures her cheerfulness;
And what serves much to her contentment,
Is to see Médée without resentment.

#### Créon.

And which god so propitious calmed her courage?

#### Cléone.

Jason, and his children, that she leaves you as pledges.
The pardon that madame obtains for them from you

Calmed the transports of her jealous spirit.                1120
The richest present that was in her power
Unites her recognition with her gratitude.
Her gown without parallel, and on which we see
From the Sun her ancestor shine a thousand rays, [35]
What the princess herself had so much wished,
By these little heroes to her just was brought,
And makes clearly visible the marvelous effects
That benefactions produce on an inflamed heart.

Créon.

Ah well, what do you say about it? What more have we to fear?

Pollux.

If you fear nothing, how I find pity for you!               1130

Créon.

Such a rare present shows a healing spirit.

Pollux.

I had always held in suspicion the gifts of enemies.
They do often enough what their weapons could not;
I know of Médée both the spirit and the spells,
And intend properly to expose myself to the cruelest demise,
If this exceptional present is no mortal allurement.

Créon.

Her children so cherished who serve for us as hostages,
Can they bestow upon us some gift of shadows?

Pollux.

Perhaps against them her treason extends,
And she no longer takes them except as belonging to Jason,   1140
Imagines herself, in hatred of their father,
Being no longer his wife, that she no longer is their mother.
Send it back, seigneur, this pernicious gift,
And burden yourself not with a precious poison.

#### Cléone.

Madame however is utterly ravished by it,
And to see herself adorned in it she burns with longing.

#### Pollux.

Where peril equals and surpasses pleasure,
One must force oneself, and vanquish one's desire.
Jason, in his love, has too much complaisance
To suffer such a gift to be accepted in his presence.        1150

#### Créon.

Without putting anything at risk, dexterously shall I know how
To reconcile your suspicions and her contentment.
We will see as early as this evening, on a criminal,
If this present hides a mortal ambush from us.
Nise, for her felonies destined to die,
Can by this trial unjustly perish;
Happy one, if her death renders us this service,
Of discovering for us in it baneful artifice!
Let us go there straight away, and consume
Neither time nor speech longer in superfluous debates.        1160

## Scene IV.

*Ægée, in prison.*

Hideous dwelling of the guilty,
Accursèd places, fatal residence,
In which never, before my love,
Sceptres were suitable.
Redouble powerfully your mortal terror,
And unite to my ailments such a lively attack,
That my soul hunted, or fleeing from fear,
Steals from my vanquishers the torture of a king.
The sad good fortune to which I aspire!
I want only to hasten my death,        1170
And accuse my bad fate
Only of suffering me still to breathe.

Since I must die, may I die as I will;
The blow would be gentle to me, if it is without infamy:
To take the order to die from an enemy hand,
Is, for a king, to die many times more than once.
Unfortunate prince, scorned thou art
When thou stoppest to serve:
If thou strivest to carry her off,
Thy prison follows thine undertaking.                                    1180
Thy love that is disdained and thy vain offence
At an eternal affront will soil thy memory:
The one already cost thee thy repose and thy glory;
The other will cost thee thy life and thy State.
Destiny, who punishes my audacity,
Thou hast only just rigors;
And if there are tender enough hearts
To sympathize with my disgrace,
My fire smothers half of their tenderness,
Since fully to compare my irons with my flame,[36]                       1190
An amorous old man merits more the blame
Than a monarch in prison is worthy of mercy
Cruel author of my misery,
Plague of hearts, tyrant of kings,
Whose imperious laws
Spare not even thy mother,[37]
Love, against Jason turn thy fatal arrow;
To the power of thy darts I hand over my vengeance:
Astound his pride, and show thy power
To lose equally one rival and the other.                                 1200
May an implacable jealousy
Follow his nuptial torch;
May ceaselessly a new object
Take possession of her fancy;
May Corinth in his sight accept another king;
May he see his race in his eyes butchered;
And, for the last misfortune, may he share the fate of Ægée,
And become at my age amorous like me!

## Scene V.

*Ægée, Médée.*

### Ægée.

But whence comes this deafening noise? what pale light
Dissipates these horrors and strikes my eyelids? 1210
Mortal, whoever thou mayst be, turn thy footsteps away from here,
And graciously inform me of the sentence of my death,
The hour, the place, the kind; and if thy heart sensible
To compassion can render itself accessible,
Give me the means of a generous action
That from the hands of tormenters my death liberates.

### Médée.

I come to free him from it. Fear no more, great prince;
Think only of seeing your dear province again;
*(She gives a stroke with her wand on the door to the prison, which opens at once;
and having pulled Ægée from it, she gives yet another upon his irons, which fall
off.)*
Neither grills nor bolts hold against me.
Cease, unworthy irons, to captivate a king; 1220
Is it for you to press against the arms of such a monarch?
And you, recognize Médée by this token,
And flee a tyrant whose frenzy
United your ordeal to my banishment;
With liberty take back courage.

### Ægée.

I take them both back to do you homage,
Princess, whose art propitious to the unfortunate
Performs such a miracle in opposition to my rigorous fate;
My life is at your service, as is the sceptre of Athens;
I owe both the one and the other to her who shatters my chains. 1230
If your happy rescue pulls me from danger,
I want to leave them only to avenge you;
And if I can ever with your assistance
Reach as far as the places where I am owed obedience,

54

You will see me, followed by a thousand battalions,
Upon these walls overthrown planting my pavilions,
To punish their traitor king for having banished you,
Within the blood of his own drowning his tyranny,
And placing again into your hands both Créuse and Jason,
To avenge your exile rather than my imprisonment.          1240

### Médée.

I want a vengeance both haughtier and more immediate;
Do not undertake it, your offer gives me shame:
To borrow the assistance of any human power,
With a reproach eternal would defame my hand.
Are there any of such kind, after all, who do not cede to me?
Who compels nature, has he need that they aid him?
Leave to me the care to avenge my anxieties,
And by what I did, judge what I can do;
The order is all given for it, be not at pains about it.
Tomorrow my art shall make my hatred triumph;          1250
Tomorrow I am Médée, and I draw reason
From my banishment and your prison.

### Ægée.

What! madame, must my modicum of power
Hinder the obligations of my gratitude?
My sceptre can it not be employed for you?
And will I be to you as much an ingrate as your spouse?

### Médée.

If I served you, all that I wish from it,
Is to find with you a secure retreat,
Where from my enemies neither threats nor presents
Might anymore trouble the repose of my years.          1260
Not that I fear them; war would to their confusion
Deliver them and all the earth to me;
But I hate this disorder, and do not love to see
That I must use my knowledge in order to live.

### Ægée.

The honor of receiving such a grand hostess[38]
From my past misfortunes effaces the sadness.
Dispose of a country that will live under your laws,
If you love it enough to give it kings;
If my years make you scorn not my person,
There you will share my bed and my crown:                              1270
If not, count on having over my subjects,
Just as over myself, an absolute power.
Let us go, madame, let us go; and through your guidance
Create the security that my flight demands.

### Médée.

My vengeance would have but an imperfect success:
I do not avenge myself, if I see not the result of it;
I owe to my wrath the happy hour of such a tender spectacle.
Go, prince, and in my absence fear no obstacle.
I will follow you tomorrow by a new trail.
For your security keep this ring;                                       1280
Its secret virtue, which makes you invisible,
Will render your departure in any direction peaceable.
Here, to prevent the alarm that the noise
Of your deliverance would before long have produced,
A phantom alike both in size and in face,
Whilst you flee, will fill your place.
Depart with no further tarrying, cherished prince of the gods,
And leave forever these detestable parts.

### Ægée.

I obey without rejoinder, and I part without delay.
Might your great enterprise with a prompt success                       1290
Fill our enemies with a mortal despair,
And give me soon the benefit of seeing you again!

END OF THE FOURTH ACT.[39]

# ACT V.

## Scene the first.

*Médée, Theudas.*

### Theudas.

Ah deplorable prince! ah, cruel fortune!
How I carry to Jason a new sadness!

*Médée, giving him a stroke with her wand that renders him immobile.*

Stop, miserable one, and let me know what effect
The present that I just made produced at the king's house.

### Theudas.

Gods! I am in the irons of an invisible chain!

### Médée.

Hurry, or this lengthy pause will attract my hate.

### Theudas.

Learn then the effect most prodigious
That ever vengeance offered to our eyes.                         1300
Your gown caused fear, and on Nise tested,
In spite of suspicions, without peril was found;
And this trial so skillfully assured them,
That forthwith Créuse wanted to adorn herself with it;
But scarcely has this unfortunate one put it on,
When she feels all at once a heat which is killing her:[40]
A subtle fire lights up, and its sparse firebrands
Over your fatal gift run in every direction;
Both Cléone and the king throw themselves upon her to extinguish
    it;
But (o new subject for weeping and wailing!)                     1310
This fire seizes the king; that prince in a moment
Finds himself enveloped within the same embrace.

## Médée.

Courage! at last both the one and the other must die.

## Theudas.

The flame would disappear, but the heat stays alive within them;[41]
And their charmed clothing, despite our vain efforts,
Are secret furnaces fastened to their bodies;
Whoever wants to strip them off himself skins them alive,
And this new relief is a new martyrdom.

## Médée.

What does my disloyal one say? what is he doing inside there?

## Theudas.

Jason, knowing nothing of these mischances,                    1320
Is acquitting himself of the duties of a civil friendship
To conduct Pollux beyond the walls of the city,
As he is going to return in haste to the wedding of his sister,
Of whom very soon Ménélas must be possessed;[42]
And I was going to carry to him this dreadful message.

> Médée, *gives him another stroke with her wand.*

Go, thou canst now finish thy journey.


## Scene II.

### Médée.

Is it enough, my vengeance, are two deaths enough?
Consult leisurely thy most ardent transports.
From the arms of my perfidious one to tear a wife,
Is it quenching to the fury of my soul?                        1330
Has she not already children by Jason,
On whom more plainly to avenge his treason!
Let us have mine take their place; let us immolate with joy
Those whom, to say farewell to me, Créuse sends to me again:
Nature, I can do it without violating thy law;
They come from his part, and no longer are mine.

But they are innocent; also was my brother innocent;
They are too criminal to have Jason for father;
Their demise must redouble his torment;
He must suffer as father as well as lover. 1340
But what! I have fairly against them to quicken my audacity,
Pity combats it, and puts itself in its place:
Then, ceding that place all of a sudden to my fury,
I adore the projects that were horrifying me:
From love all at once I pass to choler,
From the feelings of wife to the tenderness of mother.[43]
Cease henceforth, thoughts irresolute,
To spare children that I will see no more.
Dear fruits of my love, if I gave birth to you,
It is not only to caress a traitor: 1350
He deprives me of you, and I am going to deprive him of that.
But my pity is reborn, and comes again to defy me;
I execute nothing, and my soul wildly distracted
Between two passions remains suspended.
Let us deliberate about it no longer, my arm will resolve for it.
I lose you, my children; but Jason will lose you;
He will see you no more... Créon departs all in a rage;
Let us go to add this sad work to his demise.


## Scene III.

*Créon, servants.*


### Créon.

Far from relieving me you increase my torments;
The poison unites my garments with my body; 1360
And my skin, that with my garments your succor tears from me,
To follow your hand detaches from my bones.
See how my blood runs from it in great streams:
Rend me no more, officious tormenters;
Your pity for me is ventured enough;
Flee, or my fury will take you for Médée.
It is to advance my death rather than rescue me;
I want only myself to help myself die.

59

What! you continue, unfaithful rabble!
The more I forbid it of you, the more you rebel against me! 1370
Traitors, you will feel yet what I can do;
I will be your king, dying though I am;
If my commands have too little effect,
My rage at the least will do to make room for me:
Your cruel help must thus be paid.
*(He rids himself of them and chases them away with the blows of a sword.)*

## Scene IV.

*Créon, Créuse, Cléone.*

### Créuse.

Where do you flee from me, dear author of my days?
Do you flee the source innocent and unfortunate
From which take so many evils their frightful course?
This fire that consumes me both outside and in
Does it avenge you too little for my imprudent vows?[44] 1380
I cannot excuse my indiscreet envy[45]
Which brings death to one to whom I owe life:
But be satisfied with the rigors of my fate,
And cease to add your hate to my demise.
The heat which devours me, and that I deserved,
Surpasses in cruelty the eagle of Prométhée,
And I believe that Ixion given the choice of chastisements
Would prefer his wheel to my conflagrations.[46]

### Créon.

If thy young desire had much imprudence,
My daughter, I was to have opposed to it my defense.[47] 1390
I impute only to myself the excess of my misfortunes,
And I have part in thy fault in this way as in thy sufferings.
If I have some regret, it is not for my life,
Which the decline of years would soon have ravished from me:
The youth of thine, so beautiful, so flourishing,
Delivers to the bottom of my heart blows far more crushing.
My daughter, so this is thither that royal wedding

By which we were hoping to touch the pompous day![48]
Fate, pitiless, extinguishes the torch thereof,
And for nuptial bed thou must have a tomb!                    1400
Ah! rage, despair, destinies, fires, poisons, charms,
Turn fully against me your cruelest weapons:
If you must be quenched by the death of two kings,
Make it on my behalf so that I die twice,
Provided that my two deaths carry this mercy
Of leaving my crown to my matchless race,
And this hope so tender, which flattered me always,
To live again forever in its posterity.

### Créuse.

Cléone, support me, I stagger, I fall;
The remnants of my vigor succumb under my sufferings;      1410
I feel that I have no longer to suffer than a moment.
Do not refuse me this sad relief,
Sire, and if in you some love for me remains,
In your dying arms allow me to die.
My tears will water your mortal displeasures;
I will mix their waters with your burning sighs.
Ah! I burn, I die, I am no more than flame;
With mercy, hasten to receive my soul.
What! you draw yourself away!

### Créon.

Yes, I will not see,
As a cowardly witness, thine unworthy demise:                1420
It must, my child, it must be my hand that delivers me
From the infamous regret of having been able to survive thee.
Invisible enemy, leave with my blood.
*He kills himself with a poignard.*

### Créuse.

Run to him, Cléone; he pierces his side.

### Créon.

Go back; it is done. My child, adieu; I breathe my last,

And this last sigh puts an end to my martyrdom:
I leave to thy Jason the charge to avenge us.

Créuse.

Vain and sad comfort! Light relief!
My father...

Cléone.

He lives no more; his great soul has departed.

Créuse.

Give then to mine the same exit;                                   1430
Bring me that iron which, from his vanquishing evils,
Is already so knowing in how to cross the heart.
Ah! I feel blades, and fire, and poison all together;
What my father suffered joins itself with my afflictions.
Alas! may sweetness have a prompt death!
Hurry, Cléone, assist my feeble arm.

Cléone.

Despair not: the gods, more pitying,
To our just clamors will return exorable,[49]
And will preserve you, in spite of the poison,
Both as queen of Corinth, and as wife of Jason.          1440
He arrives, and surprised, his face changes;
I read in his pallor a secret rage,
And his astonishment is to turn to fury.

## Scene V.

*Jason, Créuse, Cléone, Theudas.*

Jason.

What do I see here, great gods! what spectacle of horror!
Wherever my eyes can carry my wandering view,
I see either Créon dead, or Créuse dying.
Do not go thee to it, beautiful soul, wait yet a while,

62

And the blood of Médée will extinguish all this fire;
Claim the sad pleasure of seeing her crime punished,
Of seeing for thee that infamous victim immolated;                     1450
And may that scorpion, upon the wound crushed,
Furnish the remedy to the evil that it has caused.


Créuse.

It must not be sought, the poison that kills me:
Leave me the good fortune to breathe my last in thy sight,
Suffer that I pleasure in it in this last moment:
My demise will make way for thy resentment;
My own cedes to the heat by which I am possessed;
I love better to see Jason than the death of Médée.
Approach, dear lover, and receive once more these transports:
But guard thyself from touching this miserable body;                   1460
This kiln, whose coals the charm either scatters or holds back,
Neglected Cléone, and devoured my father:
At the will of my rival it is contagious.
Jason, it is enough for me to die in thine eyes:
Prevent the pleasures of thine affliction that she awaits;
Attract not these fires enslaved by her hate.
Ah, what bitter torment! How dolorous to be thus brought to bay!
And how I feel deaths without once dying!


Jason.

What! you esteem me thus so cowardly as to live,
And such beautiful paths open to follow you?                           1470
My queen, if marriage could not unite our bodies,
We will unite our spirits, we will unite our two deaths;
And Caron will be seen passing by the dwelling of Rhadamante,[50]
In the same bark, both the lover and his lover.
Alas! you receive, by this charmed present,
The deplorable price of having loved me too much;
And since this gown caused your loss,
I must be punished to have offered it to you.
What! this poison spares me, and these impotent fires
Refuse to end the suffering that I feel!                               1480
Thus I must live, whilst you be ravished from me!

Just gods! what felony condemns me to life?
Is there some torment greater for my love
Than to see her die, and to suffer the day?
No, no; if by these fires my expectation is outwitted,
I have the wherewithal to free myself with the point of my sword;
And the example of the king, by his own hand pierced,
Who swims in torrents of the blood that he spilled,
Instructs sufficiently a generous courage
Of the means to brave the destiny which outrages it.                    1490

### Créuse.

If Créuse had ever over thee some power,
Abandon thyself not to the blows of despair.
Live to save thy name from this ignominy
That Créuse be dead, and Médée unpunished;
Live to keep my heart in thine afflicted heart,
And at the least die not that thou be not avenged.
Adieu: give thy hand; that, despite thy jealousy,
I carry to the home of Pluto the name of thy spouse.
Ah, suffering! It is done thereby, I die now,
And lose in this moment life with voice.                    1500
If thou lovest me…

### Jason.

          This word cuts off her speech;[51]
And I will not follow her soul which flies away!
My spirit, retained by her commandments,
Reserves still my life for worse torments!
Pardon, dear spouse, to my obedience;
My mortal displeasure defers to thy power,
And my accursèd days fully ready to triumph,
For fear of displeasing thee, that displeasure dares not choke from
    me.
Let us lose not time, let us run to the dwelling of the sorceress
To deliver by her death my imprisoned soul.                    1510
You others, meanwhile, carry away these two bodies:
Against all her demons my arms are strong enough,
And the part that your aid would have in my vengeance

Would not let me show my full loyalty to her.
Prepare only troubles, torments;
Become inventive in new tortures,
Causing her to die so many times on their tomb,
That her guilty blood be worth to them a hecatomb;[52]
And if this victim, in dying a thousand times,
Still appeases not the manes[53] of two kings,                    1520
I will be the second; and my faithful spirit
Will go down there to trouble her criminal soul,
Will go to make assemble for her punishment
Afflictions from Tityos to those of Ixion.
*(Cléone and the rest carry away the body of Créon and of Créuse, and Jason
continues alone.)*
But can I attribute to them my sacrificial death?
It is a pleasure to me, and not a torture.
To die, it is only—compared with them—to put myself away,
It is to join Créuse again, and not to avenge her.
Instruments of the fury of an insensible mother,
Unworthy offspring of my past love,                               1530
What unfortunate destiny had reserved to you
To bear her demise to the one who saved you?[54]
It is you, little ingrates, whom, against nature,
I must immolate atop their sepulchre
May the sorceress begin her suffering with this for you;
May her first torment be to see you die.
Yet what did they do, but obey their mother?


## Scene VI.

*Médée, Jason.*


Medée, *on high atop a balcony.*

Coward, thy despair is still deliberating upon it?
Lift thine eyes, perfidious one, and recognize this arm
Which already avenged thee through these little ingrates;          1540
This poignard that thou seest just hunted down their souls,
And drowned in their blood the remnants of our passionate flames.
Happy father and husband, my flight and their tomb

Leave the place empty for thy new nuptials.
Rejoice thee in it, Jason, go possess Créuse:
Thou wilt have no longer here anyone who accuses thee;
These tokens of our fires will beget no more for me
Secret reproaches at thy lack of faith.

### Jason.

Horror of nature, execrable tigress!

### Médée.

Go, blissful lover, cajole thy mistress:                           1550
To this object so dear thou owest all thy discourse;
To speak to me again, is to betray thy loves.
Go to her, go to her to recount thy rare adventures,
And against my actions oppose no insults.

### Jason.

What! thou darest to defy me, and thy brutality
Thinks to escape again my outraged arm?
Thou redoublest thy suffering with this insolence.

### Médée.

And what can thy feeble valiance do against me?
My art made thy force, and thy warrior exploits
Take as a result of my help all the laurels they have.          1560

### Jason.

Ah! this is too much to suffer from; a prompt torture is needed
For so many cruelties at last to punish thee.
More, more, let us break the door, let us break into the house;
How the torments all of a sudden make reason out of it for me.
Thy head will answer for so many barbarities.

### Médée, *in the air in a chariot pulled by two dragons.*

What does it serve to carry thyself away with these vain furies?
Spare thyself, dear spouse, from efforts that thou art wasting;
See the pathways in the air all open to me;

In this way do I fly, and abandon thee
To run to the exile that thy change ordained to me.                1570
Follow me, Jason, and find in these desolate parts
Postilions[55] like to my wingèd dragons.
At the last I did not badly employ the day
That the goodness of the king, thankfully, gave me;
My desires are contented. My father and my country,
I repent no more my having betrayed you;
With this sweetness I accept the blame for it.
Adieu, perjured one: learn to know thy wife,
Remember thee of her flight, and dream, another time,
Which is more to be feared, either her or two kings.              1580


## Scene VII.

### Jason.

O gods! This flying chariot, disappeared in the cloud,
Steals her away from her penalty, as well as from my sight;
And her impunity triumphs arrogantly
Over the aborted designs of my resentment.
Créuse, children, Médée, love, hate, vengeance,
Where must I, henceforth, look for some loyalty?
Where to follow the inhuman, and under what climes
To carry chastisements for so many assassinations?
Go, fury, execrable one, to some corner of the earth
Where thy chariot carries thee, and I will carry war there.       1590
I will learn of thy residence by thy bloody leavings,
And will follow thee to all parts through the rumor of thy felonies.
But what will this vain pursuit serve me,
If the air is a pathway always free to thy flight,
If always thy dragons are ready to lift thee away,
If always thy felonies have the means to defy me?
Unfortunate one, squander not against such audacity
The impotent threat of thy just fury;
Race not toward thy shame, and flee the chance
Of augmenting her victory and thy confusion.                     1600
Miserable! perfidious one! so thus thy weakness
Spares the sorceress, and betrays thy princess!

Is that the power that her desires have over thee,
And thy obedience to her last sighs?
Avenge thyself, poor lover, Créuse commands it;
Refuse her not the blood that she demands;
Listen to the tones of her dying voice,
And fly with nothing to fear of what thou owest her.
To he who knows fully how to love nothing is impossible.
Hadst thou for retreat an inaccessible rock, 1610
Tigress, thou wilt die; and despite thy knowledge,
My love will see thee submissive to its power;
My eyes will feast upon the horrors of thine affliction:
Thus Créuse wants it, thus my hatred wants it.
But what! I listen to you, impotent warm feelings!
Go, add no more full measure to my misfortunes.
To undertake a death that heaven reserves to itself,
Is to prepare again a triumph for Médée.
Turn with more effect on thyself thine arm,
And punish thyself, Jason, to punish her not. 1620
Vain transports, wherein fruitlessly my despair wastes itself,
Cease to detain me from rejoining Créuse.
My queen, my beautiful soul, in departing from these parts,
Left me vengeance, and I leave it to the gods;
They alone, whose power equals justice,
Can accomplish the torture of the sorceress.
Find it good, dear shadow, and pardon my fires
If I am going to see thee again earlier than thou wantest.
(*He kills himself.*)

END OF THE FIFTH AND FINAL ACT.

# Notes

## Act I

[1] A river in Colchos, or Colchis, where Médée's father Aeëtes, or Æëtes was king. His name is spelled Aiétès or Aéetès in French.

[2] Implored

[3] Going against what is intended

[4] Pélie (pay-LEE) or Pelias is the half brother of Jason's father Aeson (AY-son) and his rival.

[5] Acaste is the slaughtered Pélie's son.

[6] Perhaps a double entendre: figuratively, he is paying his court to a woman; literally, he means to make or establish his new royal court as a future king by marrying her.

[7] Perhaps another double entendre: Jason is both betraying Medea to rescue his children and supported or rescued against further self-reproach by needing to rescue them.

[8] The god of marriage and of the bridal hymn.

[9] A river in Hades, the underworld of ancient Greek belief.

[10] Three female spirits of justice, retribution, vengeance.

[11] The fury associated with jealous rage.

[12] That is, likely, having lost her, though possibly having married her.

## Act II

[13] Implicitly, with life, with the world

[14] Zéthès (in English, Zetes) and Calaïs are sons of Boreas, the North Wind, and a daughter of a king of Athens, and were two of the Argonauts who accompanied Jason on his quest for the Golden Fleece. They are known as the Boreads, and were turned into winds upon their death at the hands of Hercules. Castor is Pollux's twin brother and another of the Argonauts. Orpheus helped the Argonauts pass by the islands where the Sirens lived, by singing and playing louder than their voices could penetrate. He was said to have fallen in love with Calaïs, though his marriage to Eurydice and attempt to retrieve her from the underworld after her death is better known. Nestor, also one of the Argonauts, is better remembered from the *Iliad* where as an elder warrior he is an advisor to Achilles, Agamemnon and Antilochus, and from the *Odyssey* where he hosts Telemachus in the latter's quest for his father.

[15] This appears to be a reference to the second meaning of nuptials (*hyménée*), which refers to the conjugal union of the married couple, and by extension, their fertility.

[16] Jupiter, or Zeus

[17] Anchise, or Anchises, was the father of Aeneas (the title character in Virgil's *Aeneid*) through his love affair with Venus (Aphrodite). Anchises was part of the royal family at Troy. His daughter-in-law, coincidentally, was also named Créuse or Creusa; Adonis was also a lover of Venus's, as well as Proserpine's or Persephone's.

## Act III

[18] Archaic meaning: information, news

[19] Jason seems to be alluding to acquiring a dowry for her to offer to a king in exchange for marriage.

[20] Manes (pronounced MAY-nees) are the souls of the dead, considered divinities or like divinities; ancestors or relatives living in the afterworld.

[21] Catching up to him, nearly close enough to touch him

[22] As in, a better half, a second wife

[23] A very simple headband worn by a princess

[24] Or "deeds thou has performed." Corneille uses *coups d'effort* here.

[25] Also in the sense of lawful, legal.

[26] The "her" Médée refers to here is Fortuna, the Roman goddess of fortune, or perhaps luck, chance, or fate.

[27] This line seems to convey a double entendre regarding her ability both to control men's minds in the purest, most philosophical sense and to "handle" a man's earthly (and implicitly sexual) pleasures, whims, fancies, caprices (including swaying him to become besotted with her). The term for "will" is pluralized, indicating the latter but incorporating the former.

[28] Exchange, barter, bargain

[29] Fate, or La Parque in the French, refers to the Roman concept of the Fates better known to us through Greek legends. It can refer to all three of the sisters or just one. Here and below, it seems to refer to Morta, known in Greek belief as Atropos, who cuts the thread of life.

## Act IV

[30] Cave

[31] Spell

[32] Nesse, or Nessus, is a centaur killed by Hercules, whose blood later causes Hercules's death in a manner very similar to what Médée has planned for Créuse; the hydra is a water serpent with many heads.

[33] Althée, or Althaea, was a sister of Leda, one of the women with whom Jupiter, or Zeus, had a liaison as made famous by William Butler Yeats. Althaea was the mother of a man whom the Fates ordained would live until a particular firebrand was completely consumed by fire. At first putting out the fire so that her son would have a long life, she reignited it after her son

killed his uncles, killing him.

[34] A river of fire in Hades.

[35] Médée is the Sun's granddaughter.

[36] Of passion

[37] A reference to Cupid (Eros) and his mother Venus (Aphrodite).

[38] Guest, though there seems to be a double entendre in that he wishes her to become his queen, in which role, she would serve as his hostess.

[39] Ægée's final line is potentially filled with additional meanings or implications, as the word for benefit (*bien*) in French signifies not only "good," but a "right" (that is, the right to do or have something) as well as "property."

## Act V

[40] The word for heat here means also ardor, a reference to her passion for Jason.

[41] This line has significant double meaning: it might just as easily be translated as "the passion would disappear, but the ardor dwells within them," indicating that Médée has chosen for them a death fitting her assessment of their crime of obeying their passions rather than doing what is right. Those who live by the "heat" of passion will die by its heat.

[42] In French, this line is more direct, saying that Menelaus will be the "possessor" of Pollux's sister. ! This, of course, has great significance, as Pollux's sister was Helen of Troy, and Menelaus's literal and figurative ownership claim over her to the chagrin of Paris, to whom Aphrodite later promises Helen, sets off the great Trojan War.

[43] The more general "woman" may be intended here rather than wife.

[44] In French, the word used here means both vows and wishes, alluding simultaneously to her desire to have Jason despite his wife and her marriage vows.

[45] In French, the word used here (*envie*) can be used to mean envy, longing, or desire, and here seems to refer to all three.

[46] Ixion was a king from the region of Thessaly, possibly a demi-god, whom Zeus bound to a wheel of fire for all eternity to punish him for crimes against hospitality and for lusting after Zeus's wife Hera. For stealing fire from the gods and giving it to human beings, Prometheus was condemned to be chained to a rock and have his innards eaten every day by an eagle. Being an immortal, his torture was thus intended to last forever.

[47] That is, his defense of her honor and her person.

[48] An apparent reference to the Sun.

[49] Able to be persuaded or moved by pleading

[50] Caron, or Charon, is the man who ferried the souls of the dead to the underworld, Hades. Rhadamante, or Rhadamanthus, is a semi-divine king

who becomes one of the judges of their souls.

[51] In French, the word cutting off her speech is "love": if thou me lovest, syntactically.

[52] A great public sacrifice to the gods (usually a specific one), as of livestock upon an altar

[53] See above, Act III, scene III.

[54] A reference to the children's bearing of the gift of the gown to Créuse.

[55] One who rides as a guide on the near horse of one of the pairs attached to a coach or post chaise especially without a coachman

Made in the USA
Coppell, TX
21 January 2022